<u>About me</u>

This is my second book that I chose to publish through Amazon.com.

My life has been filled with challenges and adversities but I have always gotten back up again.

I have always tried to live honestly, respectfully and lovingly. In my early 20's I started experimenting with words and wrote some poems that I do not remember and that I don't have in my possession. It really took off when I started a webpage and was offering my services to people who where going divorce and for people wanting my services as a Reiki Healer. I started publishing my poetry on my webpage and didn't think much of it until someone very special to me said that I should be a poet.

Those words made it possible for me to write more poems as I wanted to express how I felt about her, I wanted to paint art in to her heart through my words, which I did.

Again, I didn't think much of it until another special person told me that I should publish them because she liked them.

I decided to do that and now I am doing it again.

With this volume I am cementing myself as one of Sweden's best poets and that I am not a one hit wonder but the wondrous master or words of love.

In gratitude, love and light

Niko Duraku

Poet, hahahahaaah

<u>Love letter</u>

Each day

My heart sings

My heart cries

My heart laughs

My heart longs

My heart yearns

My heart dreams

My heart is life

In life is love

In love I am

I

Love

You

<u>Air, version 1</u>

Ton souffle à donné un sens à mà vie.

Ton toucher et ton amour m'ont redonné vie.

L'innocence d'un d'amour pour la rose de ma vie.

Grandissant jour après jour grâce à la douceur de ton amour.

Je suis amoureux.

Tu es amoureuse.

Je t'aime.

Tu es le rayon de lumière dans ma vie.

<u>Air, version 2</u>

Your breath gave meaning to my life.

Your touch and your love brought me back to life.

The innocence of a love for the rose of my life.

Growing day by day thanks to the sweetness of your love.

I'm in love.

You are in love.

I love you.

You are the ray of light in my life.

<u>My love</u>

You

That always

And

In all ways

Will be loved

I dare not to call you mine

I dare only to dream for you to call me thine

Beauty is your name

Flowering in the presence of God

Shame

Cannot keep you down

Let your wings lift you up

To the heavens

That is in my heart

To the kingdom of love

To the sea of wisdom

The eternity of infinite realities

Always love

To be

In love

In all ways

Touched

By your heart

Your warmth

Your smile

Your shadows

Your light

Touched

To tears

Longing for just one touch

That sends ripples to my heart

Ripples of awakening

In to universal awareness

That love

Is a touch of the beloved

Wanting nothing more than to be held

Holding the dream of a touch so pure

Caressed

<u>Clarity</u>

In my eyes I see only magic

In my heart I hold only fire

In my soul I dwell in passion

On my name I hear only you

On my journey I see only you

Yes

Yes

And in infinity there are only eyes of magic

Reflected by your light

Echoed in your laughter

Passionately heart heard in the palm of my hand

Caressed gently as the breeze of my love

Dancing away in elegance

Burning

Yearning

Holding

Freedom with a kiss

Blissful heart in the art of love

Fighting in the shadows of war

Lightning strikes for each breath I take

Gazing into your eyes

That tell no lies

Love life

Life is you

Living love

<u>Soul heals</u>

Morning of glory

take away any worry

bring me to rest

in the arms of love

in beloveds heart

Dreams of the innocence of laughter

your breath

your closed eyes

your sweet peaceful sleep

reality of dreams waiting

wanting only to love

wishing for truth

freeing in the light of your smile

tears of joy

recognizing the truth of my love for my beloved

seeing me loving the honesty in your being

in

love

<u>Link</u>

Whispers of thought

temptation of the heart

pride of being humbled by love

warmed of a word

moved

touched

inspired

lightness of touch

rawful love

peacefully movement changing resilience

silence in winds of joy

loud beating of the patient lesson in life of all that ever will be

Love

<u>Beauty</u>

Wait

My shoulder is bare

And why can I not dare to

Naked in the field of dreams

Feeling the breeze of Gods breath

Warmth

Alive

Free

A lone and bare shoulder in the eyes of you

Breathing in ease with a half breath

Is it trust or is it fear that captures my lungs

In silence speaks the color of the voiceless echoes

Here

The look for those who care

A teaching of life in its loneliness

Slowly are growing in the wings of eternity

Unity in harmony and still empty

Filled

Take a breath when the breeze is on your face

Release the breaths of tomorrow' s illusions

Dream on like the love that is in the fullness of magic

Smile

The sun never outshines the beauty of the beloved in the arms of the lover

Intertwined in trust

For now there is nothingness in everything

In all is yet one

Heart

Capture the wind and the life is then again

Breathing

<u>Majestic</u>

Roads taking a step within a leap

Light shining on the corner of my journey

Wind blowing the leaf dancing the dance of death

Whistling the song of hardship

A wary head carries the melody of loneliness

Yet the heart is heard of the field of sunshine

The touch of lovers caress

Whisper in the wind

In the soul

The moon shines light to each corner of the street

Yet it shines not like the gentleness of gratitude

The power of humility

The divinity of trust

The superiority of happiness

The eternal

Within

Infinity of laughter

The depth of surrender

Take your time to be alive

Living for each moment given

In the race of what is taken

Will never be handed without force

Freedom is what is

In it is struggle

Is empowerment

Is integrity

Yet without any bounds breaths what will forever be

A life

Alive

Living in timeless spaces without laws of greed

Laws of fault

Laws of guilt

Of shame

Naked in seeing truth with celestial glow

Time will pass as it did today and the day before tomorrow

Still is lost the reason when walking the roads that leads to corners that have an end

Eternal is the bliss of reason

Infinite is the blindness in dark roads trailing for the future

All is now

All is one

One is love and so it is

So will it pass

To be passed for each beginning in birthing life

Ending not in the passing of life

Only in being where one is a lie

Imaginary illusions of false images full of mirages mirroring the falseness of one

All is here

Stillness

Oneness in one

Each moment of light is shun when it is seen with heart full of whispering
gratefulness.

<u>Trance</u>

Somewhere over the rainbow

is a heart that shines

in the breath of living

one beat to the rhythm of eternity

dancing in everlasting tranquility.

<u>Moment</u>

Power of the free

Power of the light

Too many have you been that have sought what is not

Build

Earn

Rebuild

War

Destruction

Division

Power

Why are you so subtle but yet so visible?

Why are you so sweet?

When all you stand for is hate

When love becomes the guide to which we shall strive

Power, you can never be born and you can never win because tomorrow another will come to claim you.

What is truth to those that fall victim to your illusions?

When will the light be shunned on the masks that you have worn?

Masks that only changes faces, places yet still leave the same traces.

Death

Desperation

Devouring in to the hole

Another rise but love will never fall.

<u>Music</u>

Of all the beauty and wonder

A heart of gold and light will move me yonder to dreams of life

There is much beauty to behold

None hold such beauty as a heart wanting to shine

Not for them

Not for others

Not for us

There is much shadows in the hearts of innocence

To cast some light to the heart of might is pure delight

To trust

To dare

To be willing to share

Beauty comes in the act of little magic

True love comes from the beauty within

That wish to see that in me, in you and in all

Catching a fallen innocence to hold and cherish

To set free in the whirlwind of life

In the storm of love

To sing in the name of all that is divine

To shine in what always will be beauty in the hands of the beautiful

Embraced by the comfort of treasure

Warm

<u>Nakedness</u>

There is strength in saying to someone that strength, light and love is within them.

There is humility in seeing that strength within one self.

There is fortune in those that step into their shadow to meet the light.

There is salvation of self for divinity within when faith and trust is taken in each step in blindness but sight of love and light in heart.

<u>Simplicity</u>

Time is now.

Life is now.

Joy is now.

Be what is.

Now!

<u>Heaven</u>

I am a piece of the art known as God

Crafted from love

For love

In love

In joy

Blissful heart that will never part from what is true

Yet we do not speak

We stay silent when we talk

Listening to the shouting's of our hearts

With only one voice

The voice of God

The sound of love

The presence of eternity

The inauguration of timeless levels on colors

Not only the duality of illusion

Only and always the essence of you and me, he and she of I

Hide the waves of splendor and crash into the ocean of wisdom

Here and for after

With joy and without laughter

Touch...

<u>Freedom</u>

Those that will fly with you by your side will.

Connections are not meant to be pushed or pursued only to be attracted by the willingness and desire to be.

To leave the fear of becoming and accepting the flight of life without taking a fight or in avoidance of flying on.

In love with the presence of life within the signature of what is.